Pebble® Plus
Bilingüe/
Bilingual

Tiburones/Sharks

Tiburón mako/Mako Shark

por/by Deborah Nuzzolo

Editor Consultor/Consulting Editor: Dra. Gail Saunders-Smith

Consultor/Consultant: Jody Rake, member
Southwest Marine/Aquatic Educators' Association

CAPSTONE PRESS
a capstone imprint

Pebble Plus is published by Capstone Press,
151 Good Counsel Drive, P.O. Box 669, Mankato, Minnesota 56002.
www.capstonepress.com

092009
005618CGS10

 Books published by Capstone Press are manufactured with
paper containing at least 10 percent post-consumer waste.

Library of Congress Cataloging-in-Publication Data
Nuzzolo, Deborah.
    [Mako shark. Spanish & English]
    Tiburón mako = Mako shark / por/by Deborah Nuzzolo.
    p. cm. — (Pebble plus bilingüe/bilingual. Tiburones/sharks)
    Includes index.
    Summary: "Simple text and photographs present mako sharks, their body parts, and their behavior —
in both English and Spanish" — Provided by publisher.
    ISBN 978-1-4296-4803-5 (library binding)
    1. Mako sharks — Juvenile literature. I. Title. II. Title: Mako shark. III. Series.
QL638.95.L3N88318 2010
597.3'3 — dc22   2009037912

Editorial Credits
Megan Peterson, editor; Strictly Spanish, translation services; Katy Kudela, bilingual editor;
    Ted Williams, set designer; Kyle Grenz, book designer; Jo Miller, photo researcher;
    Eric Manske and Danielle Ceminsky, production specialists

Photo Credits
Alamy/Stephen Frink Collection, 4–5; Visual&Written SL, cover, 9, 10–11
Bruce Coleman Inc./Maris Kazmers, 1
Corbis/Amos Nachoum, 7
Getty Images Inc./Visuals Unlimited/Richard Herrmann, 13
Nature Picture Library/Doug Perrine, 19
Seapics/Caterina Gennaro-Kurr, 16–17; Richard Herrmann, 15, 20–21
Shutterstock/Simone Conti, backgrounds

Note to Parents and Teachers

The Tiburones/Sharks set supports national science standards related to the
characteristics and behavior of animals. This book describes and illustrates mako sharks
in both English and Spanish. The images support early readers in understanding the text.
The repetition of words and phrases helps early readers learn new words. This book also
introduces early readers to subject-specific vocabulary words, which are defined in the
Glossary section. Early readers may need assistance to read some words and to use the
Table of Contents, Glossary, Internet Sites, and Index sections of the book.

Table of Contents

Tabla de contenidos

Fast Sharks

What is the fastest

shark in the sea?

It's the mako shark.

Tiburones veloces

¿Cuál es el tiburón

más veloz del mar?

Él es el tiburón mako.

Mako sharks live worldwide
in warm and cool water.
They swim along the shore
and in deeper water.

Los tiburones mako viven en todas
partes del mundo en aguas templadas
y frías. Ellos nadan a lo largo de
la orilla y en aguas más profundas.

What They Look Like

Two kinds of mako sharks dash through the sea. They are shortfin makos and longfin makos.

A qué se parecen

Dos tipos de tiburones mako nadan rapidísimo en el mar. Son los mako de aleta corta y los mako de aleta larga.

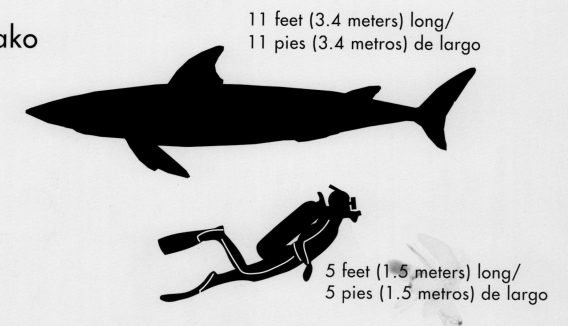

11 feet (3.4 meters) long/
11 pies (3.4 metros) de largo

5 feet (1.5 meters) long/
5 pies (1.5 metros) de largo

Shortfin makos have shorter pectoral fins than longfin makos. These fins help sharks steer like wings on an airplane.

Los mako de aleta corta tienen aletas pectorales más cortas que los mako de aleta larga. Estas aletas ayudan a los tiburones a navegar como las alas en un avión.

**pectoral fins/
aletas pectorales**

Mako sharks have

large black eyes.

They see well in dim light.

Los tiburones mako tienen

ojos grandes y negros.

Ellos ven bien en luz tenue.

13

Mako Shark Pups

Mako shark eggs

hatch inside the mother.

Between four and 16 pups

are born at one time.

Crías del tiburón mako

Los huevos del tiburón mako se

incuban dentro de la madre.

Nacen entre cuatro y 16

crías al mismo tiempo.

15

Hunting

Mako sharks hunt tuna, mackerel, and swordfish.

Caza

Los tiburones mako cazan atún, caballa y pez espada.

The mako shark uses

its strong tail

to zoom after prey.

El tiburón mako usa su fuerte

cola para nadar rápidamente

detrás de su presa.

19

Mako sharks attack

with sharp, hooklike teeth.

They are swift hunters.

Los tiburones mako atacan con

dientes filosos en forma de ganchos.

Ellos son cazadores veloces.

Glossary

dim — not very bright

hunt — to chase and kill animals for food

pectoral fin — the hard, flat limb on either side of a shark

prey — an animal hunted by another animal for food

pup — a young shark

shore — the place where the water meets land; many sharks swim in the shallow water near the shore.

steer — to move in a certain direction

swift — moving or able to move very fast

Internet Sites

FactHound offers a safe, fun way to find Internet sites related to this book. All of the sites on FactHound have been researched by our staff.

Here's all you do:

Visit *www.facthound.com*

FactHound will fetch the best sites for you!

Glosario

la aleta pectoral — miembro plano y duro a cada lado del tiburón

cazar — perseguir y matar animales para comer

la cría — un tiburón joven

navegar — mover a un objeto en cierta dirección

la orilla — el lugar donde el agua se junta con la tierra; muchos tiburones nadan en el agua poco profunda cerca de la orilla.

la presa — un animal cazado por otro para comérselo

tenue — que no es brillante

veloz — que se mueve o es capaz de moverse muy rápidamente

Sitios de Internet

FactHound brinda una forma segura y divertida de encontrar sitios de Internet relacionados con este libro. Todos los sitios en FactHound han sido investigados por nuestro personal.

Esto es todo lo que tú necesitas hacer:

Visita *www.facthound.com*

¡FactHound buscará los mejores sitios para ti!

Index

Índice